A Fun Place to Eat

Written by Beth Jenkins Grout
Illustrated by Linda Weller

Adams 12 Five Star Schools
1500 E 128th Avenue
Thornton, CO 80241
(720) 972-4000

I want a fun place to eat!

3

I do not want to sit still.

I want to spin in my chair.

I want to flip my spoon.

I want to clap my hands.

7

8 I want to stamp my feet.

I want an ice cream float.

And so…

Mom and Dad took me to a
new place to eat.

I got to spin in my chair.

I got to flip my spoon.

13

I got to clap my hands.

I got to stamp my feet.

And I got an ice cream float.